# American Foundations
## LAID BY THE BAPTISTS

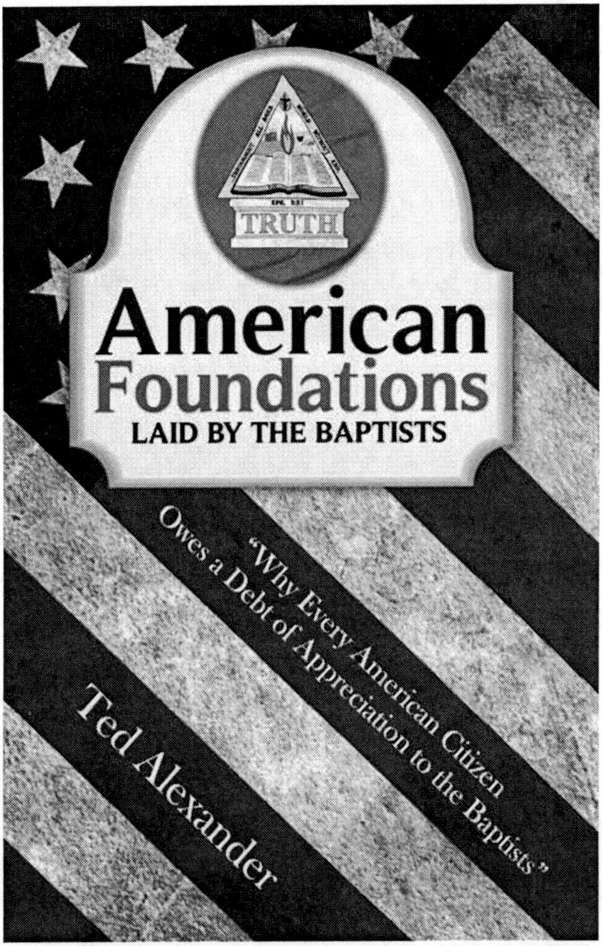

*"Why Every American Citizen Owes a Debt of Appreciation to the Baptists"*

Ted Alexander

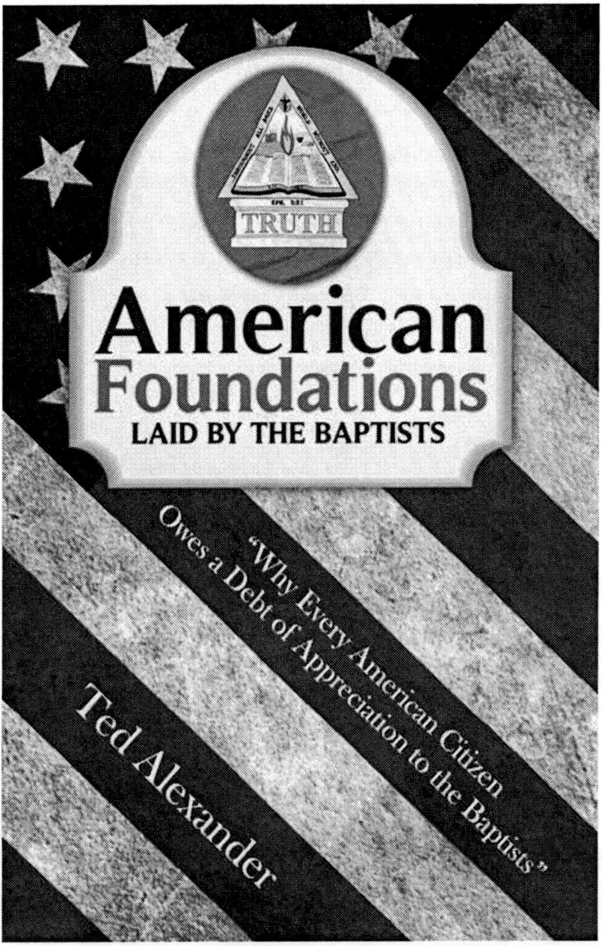

# American Foundations
## LAID BY THE BAPTISTS

"Why Every American Citizen Owes a Debt of Appreciation to the Baptists"

Ted Alexander

BAPTIST TRUTH PUBLISHING

Copyright © 2015 Ted Alexander. All rights reserved.

Writings contained herein are by the author unless otherwise stated.

No part of this publication may be reproduced, stored in a retrieval system or transmitted in any way by any means – electronic, mechanical, photocopy, recording or otherwise – without the prior permission of the copyright holder, except as provided by USA copyright law.

All Scriptures are taken from the King James Bible.

ISBN# 978-1-61119-143-1

Printed in the United States of America.

Printed by Calvary Publishing
A Ministry of Parker Memorial Baptist Church
1902 East Cavanaugh Road
Lansing, Michigan 48910
www.CalvaryPublishing.org

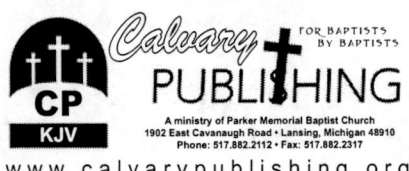

www.calvarypublishing.org

# Contents

Acknowledgements . . . . . . . . . . . . . . . . 7

Introduction . . . . . . . . . . . . . . . . . . . . . . 9

The Birth, Growth, And Health Of America: It Was No "Accident!" . . . . 11

    The Spiritual Foundations Of America Were Laid By The Baptists . . . . . . . 17

    The Political Foundations Of America Were Laid By The Baptists . . . . . . . . 35

    The Foundations Of The American Revolution Were Laid By The Baptists . . . . . . . . . . . . . . . . . . . . . . . 73

Conclusion . . . . . . . . . . . . . . . . . . . . . . 89

Afterword . . . . . . . . . . . . . . . . . . . . . . 91

Works Cited . . . . . . . . . . . . . . . . . . . . 95

Photographs . . . . . . . . . . . . . . . . . . . . 98

# Acknowledgements

*I want to take a moment to thank my precious wife Jodi who has been the best helpmeet, proofreader, constructive critic, thinker, and friend I could have ever asked for. Her keen insight, knowledge of English grammar, and her overall encouragement on this and many previous projects is invaluable. Thank you, Sweetie.

*I also want to thank my pastor, Travis Burke. He is a friend, a wonderful pastor, a faithful proofreader, and a constant encourager in my endeavors.

*In Memorial: I want to acknowledge my former pastor James Beller. Brother Beller gave me a lot of encouragement personally. Brother Beller went to Heaven in March of 2014, but he was alive when this project started and he gave me inspiration that pushed me toward writing this book. Many times he offered direction on how to proceed with my writing ministry. I called on Brother Beller to speak on our Baptist Heritage Revival Tours on several occasions, and he never failed to bring us Spirit-filled, well-researched, helpful messages. I thank God for Brother Beller's leadership, friendship and camaraderie in the monumental task of giving Baptist people their heritage back. He is greatly missed.

# Introduction

**Weighty And Vital Assertions**

The book you are reading was written to accomplish two specific goals. The first goal of the author is to explain America's overall greatness when compared with that of the other nations in the world. The prosperity, strength, and spirituality of the "Land of Liberty" has allowed it to stand head and shoulders above all other nations for a very long time. When one compounds that with the superior form of government that is unique to America, one begins to realize why this nation is viewed by so many as the envy of much of the world.

That being said, it must be understood that the source of America's principles of liberty and of her spirituality is not a mystery. The many strengths of the United States have definite and distinct origins. The means of America's formation, progress, and greatness can easily be seen and understood when one simply looks at America from a Christian perspective. America cannot be fully comprehended until it is viewed through the lens of the Holy Scriptures.

The second goal of this book is to correct the false historical narratives being passed off by both religious and secular forces. Anti-Americanism, secularism, and the pagan Catholic and Catholic-reformed worldviews have caused great violence to the testimony of the Baptists. The true history of America has been misconstrued and twisted to the extent that even the Gospel itself has suffered.

In order to reach these two goals, it will be important to understand many pertinent facts concerning America that are largely unknown and, thus, rarely discussed.

The strength of this book will hinge on one major truth: namely, that without the scriptural churches of the Lord Jesus Christ, the America that the world knows today would not exist in its current form and may, perhaps, not exist at all.

The major principle represented in the titling of this book is that American foundations have been laid by the Baptists; and due to this fact, America and the world owe a great debt of gratitude to the Baptists.

The author realizes that due to the prevailing ignorance of our generation, to many these statements will come across as reckless. The author will now begin to prove these assertions beyond any shadow of a doubt.

# The Birth, Growth, And Health Of America: It Was No "Accident!"

That's right, dear reader, America was no accident. Its birth was no accident; its growth was no accident; and its current state of prosperity and liberty is not an ongoing accident either. The reason America has prospered in so many ways above that of other nations is because America has been blessed by God. The Bible states in Proverbs 14:34, "Righteousness exalteth a nation: but sin is a reproach to any people." The reason that America has been exalted is because so many righteous people have lived in America. If large groups of people live righteously, that people group will be exalted. This is exactly how America obtained great favor with God.

The Bible further states in Psalms 33:12, "Blessed is the nation whose God is the Lord; and the people whom he hath chosen for his own inheritance." While it is abundantly clear that this verse of Scripture is referencing the nation of Israel, the Bible believer can also assume that, in principle, it would apply to any nation. The author therefore does not find it to be a stretch to state that America has been blessed and is blessed today to a large degree because God has been the Lord of so many lives in America.

## Think Logically: How Would A Christian Think America Became Great If It Were Previously Unknown To Him?

To really see the wisdom in crediting Christ's Baptist churches with America's greatness, the reader is asked here to consider the following scenario. Assuming that the reader is a Baptist or at the very least identifies himself as a Christian, you are hereby entreated to think about America as though it were an unheard of land that you were visiting for the very first time. Please try to play along for sake of allowing the author to make an immensely important point. Imagine you stumbled upon this nation and didn't even know its name. After being here for a short time you would very quickly notice the immeasurable degree of liberty that every citizen of this country enjoys. When you consider this, you realize that this flood tide of liberty is not flowing in other nations nearly to the degree that it does in America. The next thing you would notice is the abundant wealth and prosperity in this strange place. It would become quite obvious that this is not a land of poverty as many other nations are, but a land of an overwhelming abundance of material blessings. In fact, you would quickly find out that America is so prosperous that it turns around and feeds many other nations of the world with its overflow of food. In addition, you would discover that America financially gifts many other nations annually. Then you would examine the military might of this nation and see that it is colossal! This country also has a history of victory in many great battles, you are told. Here it dawns on you, and you begin to realize why they called it the last existing "Superpower." You would evidence modern medicine, institutions of higher education, and charities for the poor. In fact, there are thousands upon thousands of churches, hospitals, schools, and modern conveniences found in America. Then you would turn to recognize the history of America's love for life and humanity. This nation you stumbled upon has helped to liberate many other nations and has even rebuilt nations that it was forced to destroy during the course of horrible wars.

If you, dear reader, were to stumble upon a nation such as this, which seems to be blessed so greatly, you would probably not have to wonder how this happened. As a Christian, you would be forced to assume that at some point in time the true churches of the Lord Jesus Christ have had to have done ample work here and therefore had a sweeping influence on this land-and you would be exactly right! Righteousness has exalted this nation! But that righteousness was not an abstract force in and of itself. It was the churches of the Lord Jesus Christ who preached and practiced that righteousness that have caused the blessings of God to fall upon this nation.

Do not err. It is not that this nation has been blessed because God is the Lord of so many people's lives in America in some generic sort of way. Rather, America has been blessed specifically because God has been the Lord over so many Baptist people's lives. This thesis is not an assumption, nor guesswork, nor wishful thinking; it is an historical fact! This fact will be proven within this dissertation.

Truly the blessings all over America are derived and overflow blessings. In other words, God has blessed America because there were so many scriptural churches here, and those scriptural churches have incurred the blessing of God on them. Jesus is only working in and through one institution on planet Earth, and that institution is His New Testament church.

The author loves a tasty, home cooked, fried chicken dinner. The best way he has found to celebrate such a nearly perfect meal is to smother the mashed potatoes with homemade gravy. It just so happens that the chicken gets a secondary dousing, along with the green beans. In fact, usually the whole plate is covered with a generous portion of mouth-watering gravy, if everything works out right. This is what happened to the United States of America. God has blessed, used, empowered, and poured out His Spirit upon His churches as they served Him, and the whole land was covered with the "spiritual gravy" that God slathered all over His people. His people are the salt of the earth and the light of the world; and wherever they are, there is the presence and blessings of their God.

## Not Pride, Just A Humbling Fact

While it must be recognized that there were many non-Baptists that have contributed to the founding, health and prosperity of America, none have even approached unto the towering contributions and amazing things that the Baptists have accomplished.

## To Summarize

America has been blessed by God because God has been at work in His scriptural churches. Because there have been so many of His scriptural churches here, the blessings have overflowed to the whole of America. The Gospel the Baptists have preached all across America has changed many lives from that of worldly heathens to that of upstanding Christians. In addition, the many contributions that the Baptists have made have become the pillars and foundation of all that is great in America. Thus, America is great because of the existence and contributions of the Baptists and Baptist churches in this land.

There are three major categories in which the Baptists have positively influenced America. In these three areas, the lasting and powerful influence of the Baptists and the Lord's scriptural Baptist churches cannot be denied. The Baptists have made mammoth contributions spiritually, politically, and militarily.

# 1. The Spiritual Foundations Of America Were Laid By The Baptists

**The Great Awakening**

The certainty that the state-sponsored churches of England in their various forms were never going to bring any true spiritual life or renewal to the colonies would have been obvious to any spiritual observer of the colonial era. Any religion based on the premise that men's consciences are of no import and are inconsequential in comparison to outward religious rituals and religious systems is doomed to mislead men's souls.

However, when certain key men from within the state churches began to openly preach the pure Gospel of the Lord Jesus Christ, great things began to happen spiritually, not only in America, but also in England.

The Great Awakening, which started nearly simultaneously in both England and America, would prove to be, by far, the greatest spiritual revival the colonies had seen up to that timeframe. Through this outpouring of the Spirit, God changed the religious landscape of the colonies.

The beginnings of the revival can be traced back to the preaching ministry of Jonathan Edwards in New England and George Whitefield in his various locations. Edwards was a New England "Standing Order" preacher. As he began to preach on the great themes of judgment from the Word of God, many of the lost members in his church were spiritually awakened and began to cry out to God for salvation. This revival spilled over until at least twenty "Standing Order" churches were experiencing a move of God among their congregations. He preached things that people had rarely heard before in the state churches, such as complete surrender to the Holy Spirit and the reoccurring Biblical theme of "Ye must be born again."

Around the same timeframe, Whitefield was converted after an arduous wrestling match with the Holy Spirit. Across the ocean while studying to be an Anglican minister, he met the Wesley brothers- John and Charles. These men had a great influence on Whitefield until eventually he was heartily saved.

Whitefield preached in England, and his adherence to the Bible as his sole text was so alarming to the Anglican Church officials that the Bishop of London denounced him in 1739. Although he was ordained as an Anglican priest, he purposefully stood for truth, knowing that this would naturally cause a separation from his mother institution.

# LAID BY THE BAPTISTS

This preacher, who was initially mocked and called a child parson, began to have great success across England, and soon no one was laughing. His severance with Anglicanism was somewhat irrelevant as the crowds that were attending his preaching events could not be contained in the rather small, Anglican, church buildings. He and his converts were dubbed "New Lights" by many observers. His fame spread abroad and quickly reached the shores of America. His friend John Wesley then beckoned Whitefield to come and preach. Whitefield obliged, and he soon took his first of many trips to America. Once Whitefield began to travel to America for the purpose of preaching, his ministry arose to great heights.

Whitefield preached all across the colonies, and untold thousands were soundly converted. Crowds would throng to him as he preached over and over again. One city was changed, and then another, and then another. So many were converted to Christ under Whitefield that the historian William Lumpkin stated, "In a brief six-week period, the religious climate of New England was changed!"[1] This change that was experienced in New England was the same change that permeated most of the colonies.

---

1 William L. Lumpkin, *Baptist Foundations in the South*, reprinted (Ashville: Revival Literature, 2006), p. 4.

## Great But Not The Greatest

While most Christian historians recognize the Great Awakening as just that- "great"- most do not consider the fact that this revival was merely God's opening act in a show that was about to take religious influences in America to an entirely new level.

## The Effects Of The Great Awakening

Indeed, the Great Awakening produced multitudes of converts across the colonies and even across the ocean. In addition, the failure of the halfway covenant, which allowed for unregenerate adults and infants to become baptized members in the "Standing Order" churches, was exposed as the unscriptural and absolute failure that it truly was. The halfway covenant made it nearly impossible for "Standing Order" ministers to ever reach the true heart of man.

Another one of the effects of the Great Awakening was that the ranks of the Baptists began to swell to numbers not previously seen in the colonies. Whitefield himself, frustrated that so many of the converts of his meetings became Baptists, stated, "All my chickens have turned to ducks."[2] While it is obvious that Whitefield was not happy about this fact, it nonetheless shows the observer that the heart of many of these new converts was to study the Bi-

---
2  Ibid, p. 20

ble to find out where true religion, Biblical baptism, and the true churches really were. Whitefield likely used the analogy of chickens versus ducks because while chickens like a little bit of water, ducks fully immerse themselves and love deep water. Once Whitefield's converts came to Baptist principles, the Baptist ministers demanded they abandon their previous pouring or sprinkling, for the Scriptural, authoritative deep water baptism of the Scriptures. For sure, multitudes both inside and outside of the "Standing Order" churches heard the Gospel clearly preached for the first time in their life; and God saved many, many souls.

## The After Effects Of The Great Awakening

The Great Awakening, as grand as it was, eventually faded as God moved the center of spiritual activity almost exclusively inside the Baptist assemblies. This was an inevitable course for the great revival to take for several reasons.

The eventual decay of the Great Awakening should not surprise the thinking observer, as the seeds of its disintegration were sown early and often. To be honest with the historical record, it will be necessary to point out some of the glaring failures of this revival movement.

Firstly, the key leaders of this movement were

men with unscriptural religious training. When the revival began, George Whitefield was a Cambridge-trained, Anglican priest. The Wesley brothers attended school with Whitefield and were of the same strand. Jonathan Edwards was a "Standing Order" state-church pastor. Their understanding of what a Scriptural church was, was greatly wanting. In addition, Whitefield's severance from Anglicanism- although warranted- moved Whitefield's ecclesiological position more towards a rogue, Lone Ranger-type practice than towards that of a local church, Baptist position. Whitefield rejected a wrongful authority only to seemingly opt for no authority at all. It is sad to consider that he never became a Baptist.

Obviously, Whitefield, a "New Light" himself, often encouraged his converts to attend "New Light" churches. The glaring problem with this practice was that the "New Lights" were largely the children of Congregationalism and Puritanism. These groups had their roots in the corrupt Anglican Church of England. Had the Puritans truly desired purity, they should have demanded a complete severance from Anglicanism. They chose rather to modify it instead. So the "New Lights" were ultimately descended from Anglicanism. To go back one more generation is to discover that the mother of Anglicanism is the Roman Catholic institution.

The point of this history lesson is to show that

Whitefield was encouraging people to continue on in a strain of religion that had no biblical authority and had no past lineage or current connection to the true churches of the Lord Jesus Christ. So then the "New Lights", as much as they were attempting to separate themselves from what they knew to be false, were simply the great granddaughters of the Roman Catholic institution. Their history can be traced right back to the "MOTHER OF HARLOTS" of Revelation 17.

Because of Whitefield's training, his ecclesiological views, and his authority and origin problems, he never took the proper Biblical stand on deep-water, authoritative baptism or church membership in a legitimate, authoritative Baptist church. As proof of this, Lumpkin stated the following:

> Now the Episcopal preachers began to itinerate and to immerse adults, but they continued to complain that the people were "bewitched" by Baptist preaching. Their pamphleteering and other propaganda for infant baptism were given a boost in 1764 when George Whitefield stopped briefly in New Bern and spoke against the "rebaptism" of adults and in favor of the baptism of infants.[3]

---

3  George W. Paschal, *History of North Carolina Baptists*, Vol. 1 (Raleigh: General Board of North Carolina Baptist State Convention, 1930), p. 313.

## From The Great Awakening To The Separate Baptist Revival

By the year 1753, the effects of the Great Awakening were still being enjoyed, however, at a greatly reduced strength. It was also around this time that a transition began to take place. The time for the Lord's true churches to shine was now. In 1755, it became abundantly clear that the center of the work of the Spirit of God in America was now squarely settled in the Baptist assemblies. At this time, revival activity moved from the hands of the "New Lights", or Separates, into the hands of the Baptists, or more specifically, the newly identified Separate Baptists. The Lord would also, at this time, transition the geographical location of His outpouring. The New England states saw the greatest wave of revival under Whitefield and the "New Lights"; now the revival activity would be focused in North Carolina, Virginia, and South Carolina under Shubal Stearns and the Separate Baptists.

The key players of the revival were Shubal Stearns, Daniel and Abraham Marshall, Samuel Harriss, and Tidence Lane, among others.

## The Separate Baptist Revival

The stage was now set and what was about to take place in America among the Baptists would easily outshine the Great Awakening. Ironically, the faithful leader of the Separate Baptists, Shubal Stearns, was brought to Christ under Whitefield's preaching.

Shubal Stearns was saved in the year 1746. Before long, he became a pastor of a New Light Church. By 1751, and after being challenged by the Baptist Wait Palmer to study the issue of baptism from Scripture, he submitted to Baptist baptism at the hands of Palmer. Stearns was ordained as a Baptist minister in May of 1751 by Wait Palmer and Joshua Morse.

After pastoring as a Baptist for a few years, in 1754 Stearns left New England in a group of a dozen people, as he was looking for greater fields of service. Stearns traveled southward, stopping briefly in New York and Philadelphia. Before long this group paused in Hampshire County, Virginia. It was at this time that Stearns received word from North Carolina that there was a great need for Gospel preachers there. He read in one letter how that people were willing to ride on horseback upwards of forty miles to hear one sermon. God used this to light a fire in Shubal Stearns' heart. At this time, the Lord directed Stearns to travel southward and settle in the Sandy Creek area of north central North Carolina.

This field was closed to Whitefield, and now opened by God to the Baptists. Back in December of 1739, after Whitefield's failed attempt to bring revival to North Carolina, he wrote the following entry in his journal: "Oh God that thou would send forth a John the Baptist to preach and baptize in the wilderness."[4] Shubal Stearns was the Baptist who became the answer to Whitefield's prayer. The stage was now set and Stearns was about to set North Carolina on fire for Christ.

**A Mighty Rushing Wind**

As Shubal Stearns began to preach to the small crowd of about sixteen hearers in the fall air of North Carolina, the most Scriptural, far reaching, long lasting revival that America would ever see began.

Unlike the work of Whitefield, this work was organized and well ordered. The Bible was more carefully followed, as deep-water baptism, church membership, and church discipline were important to the Separate Baptists. Many were saved, baptized and added to the assembly at Sandy Creek. The membership of the newly birthed Sandy Creek Baptist Church in just two short years grew from sixteen to over six hundred members.

The preaching of the Baptist caused a similar effect on individuals to that of Mr. Whitefield. Only now, the salvation of the sinner was not the

---

4  George Whitefield, *George Whitefield's Journals* (Guilford and London: Banner of Truth, Billing and Sons, Ltd., 1960), p. 373.

final goal, it was just the first step of the great commission followed by biblical baptism, training and sending out preachers to start new works.

It is not an embellishment to say that the preaching of Stearns was alarming, captivating, and even shocking. Lumpkin describes Stearns as "...a matchless preacher... [initial hearers] could not decide which was more remarkable, the content or the delivery."[5] Cathcart further described Stearns in this manner: "He was eloquent, wise, humble, pathetic, full of faith, and wholly consecrated to God, and few men ever enjoyed more of the Spirit's presence in the closet and in preaching the gospel. He was undoubtedly one of the greatest ministers that ever presented Jesus to perishing multitudes, and one of the most successful soul-winners that ever unfurled the banner of Calvary."[6] Tidence Lane described his conversion under Stearns's preaching in these words:

> When the fame of Mr. Stearns' preaching reached the Yadkin where I lived, I felt a curiosity to go and hear him. Upon my arrival I saw a venerable man sitting under a peach-tree with a book in his hand and the people gathering about him. He fixed his eyes upon me immediately, which made me feel in

---

5 Lumpkin, p. 31.
6 William Cathcart, *The Baptist Encyclopedia*, Vol. 2 (Philadelphia: Louis H. Everts, 1883), p. 1100.

such a manner as I had never felt before. I turned to quit the place, but could not proceed far. I walked about, sometimes catching his eyes as I walked...My uneasiness increased and became intolerable. I went up to him, thinking that a salutation and shaking of hands would relieve me; but it happened otherwise. I began to think he had an evil eye and ought to be shunned, but shunning him I could no more effect than a bird can shun the rattlesnake when it fixes its eyes upon it. When he began to preach my perturbations increased so that nature could no longer support them and I sank to the ground.[7]

Elnathan Davis' conversion is recorded as follows:

He had heard that one John Steward, being a very big man, and Shubal Stearns of small stature, he concluded there would be some diversion if not drowning; therefore he gathered about 8 or 10 of his companions in wickedness and went to the spot. Shubal Stearns came and began to preach;... He [Elnathan] stood a while in that resolution; but the enchantment of Shubal Stearns voice drew him to the crowd once more. He had not been long there before the trem-

---

[7] Morgan Edwards, "Materials North Carolina," unpublished manuscript, p. 387.

> bling seized him also; he attempted to withdraw; but his strength and his understanding confounded, he, with many others, sunk to the ground. When he came to himself he found nothing in him but dread and anxiety, bordering on horror. He continued in this situation some days, and then found relief by faith in Christ. Immediately he began to preach conversion work, raw as he was, and scanty as his knowledge must have been.[8]

Sandy Creek saw many men saved and called to preach the Gospel of Christ. It was the manner of the Separate Baptists to train these men and send them out to birth churches as soon as they were prepared. This revival would not be just a revival of souls saved; it would be a revival of New Testament Baptist church planting.

Within seventeen years from the beginning of this move of God, the Separate Baptists had established forty-two churches from which one hundred twenty-five preachers were raised up.

Estimates vary as to the effects this revival had over the generation in which it started; however, it is believed that even a conservative estimate would indicate that by 1800, the Separate Baptists had birthed over one thousand churches in America!

Samuel Harriss, the Virginia Separate Baptist, is

---

8  Ibid, p. 391

known to have birthed around sixty churches alone, not to mention the countless other churches the Separate Baptists started in Virginia.

Daniel Marshall, brother-in-law of Stearns, was a fervent church planter and had his hand in dozens of church plants in Virginia, North Carolina, and South Carolina. He also established the first Baptist church in all of Georgia- Kiokee.

This pioneering spirit was not unusual, for Tidence Lane, the Separate Baptist, started the first Baptist church in Tennessee. Tennessee would then be flooded with Baptists to the point that Knoxville became known as "Baptist Town."

Kentucky was flooded with the influence of the Separate Baptists as men like Lewis Craig traveled there. These giants of the Baptist faith spattered churches across the countryside as though they were flinging handfuls of seeds into their garden!

Thus, the entire landscape of the South became covered and saturated with Baptist churches. This great work can be traced directly back to the doorstep of the Sandy Creek Church. Credit must be given completely to the Separate Baptists!

David Benedict recorded:

> Sandy Creek Church is the mother of all the Separate Baptists. From this Sion went forth the Word, and great was the company of them who published it, insomuch that

her converts were as drops of morning dew. This church in seventeen years has spread her branches westward as far as the great river Mississippi; southward as far as Georgia; eastward to the sea and Chesapeake Bay; and northward to the waters of the Potomac; it, in seventeen years, is become mother, grandmother, and great-grandmother, to forty-two churches, from which sprang 125 ministers.[9]

## This Revival Shaped America Spiritually For Generations To Come

The venerable Baptist historian David Cummins, before his death, communicated to the author during a telephone conversation that he believed that America's "Bible Belt" should be renamed the "Separate Baptist Belt", as it was strictly formed by the influence of the Baptists. This conclusion does make perfect sense. Since the "Bible Belt" was formed almost exclusively by the Baptists, whatever credit it has received for shaping America's moral character should rightly be attributed to Baptists. Whatever the "Bible Belt" is, it became that way through Baptist doctrine, thought, practice, and even some widely held Baptist opinion.

Of the thousands of churches that make up the

---

9 David Benedict, *A General History of the Baptist Denomination in America* (Boston: Manning and Loring, 1813), p. 1169.

"Bible Belt", an overwhelming majority are still Baptist. The conservative, Southern, political mindset that has shaped America through countless elections can be traced back to the Bible preaching of the Baptists. Even today, two and a half centuries later, the overwhelming conservative voting block rests in the cradle of the "Baptist Bible Belt."

The very reason that open public nudity is displayed across European countries but not the United States is because America had a Separate Baptist revival and therefore has a "Bible Belt." The Baptist revival has filled the South with voters that have pushed back at all sorts of sin.

The reason other nations are steeped in false cults that thrive on murder and terror, as opposed to Christianity's maxims of love and kindness is due to the fact that the other nations have no "Bible Belt."

From the "Bible Belt" region sprang thousands of missionaries throughout over two and one half centuries. These missionaries to America and dozens of foreign countries have changed the world. The modern missions movement truly started with the Baptist William Carey in England, but the explosive spread of foreign missions was not expressly seen in England nearly to the degree that it was seen in America. It is further evident that this American missions torch was carried and displayed almost exclusively by the Baptists. It started here with key

# LAID BY THE BAPTISTS 33

men like Adoniram Judson, Luther Rice, and Richard Furman, and continues to this very day. The amount of Bibles printed, shipped, circulated and gifted throughout the homeland and foreign lands is difficult to ascertain but must be considered immense. This too is a direct result of Baptist influences in the South.

This nation has recognized religious liberty, unlike other nations, and subsequently the American "Bible Belt" has been left unchecked by enemies of liberty since the ratifying of the Bill of Rights. For example, if the "Bible Belt" had seen its formation in communist Russia, communist China, or Nazi Germany, its spread and success would never have become a reality. Consider this, when was the last time the United States government so much as hindered Baptist missionaries from either entering or leaving this country? But, because the "Bible Belt" has been couched in a culture of liberty, it has blazed spiritual and political trails in every direction since the very first message Shubal Stearns preached at Sandy Creek.

## What Does It All Mean?

Based on the aforementioned facts, it would be inconceivable to even suggest that the Separate Baptist "Bible Belt" has been rivaled by any other Christian force in the entire history of the world.

The overwhelming unity in belief and action of this largely Southern conglomerate called the "American Bible Belt" will be recorded in eternity's history book as one of the greatest of spiritual forces that has existed on Earth. This powerful belt furthered the kingdom of God in a way that can truly only be measured by the Lord of the Harvest Himself! Remove the Separate Baptists from America, and you have corrupted the nation and the world in a way that they become unrecognizable to the average observer. Truly, without the Baptists, America is largely a pagan land!

# 2. The Political Foundations Of America Were Laid By The Baptists

Leviticus 25:10a says, "And ye shall hallow the fiftieth year, and proclaim liberty throughout all the land unto all the inhabitants thereof: it shall be a jubilee unto you…"

In this study of Baptist influences on America, one does not have to shift too many gears when moving his thought pattern from the spiritual contributions of the Baptists to their political contributions. There is a reason for this. To a Baptist Bible-believer, the Word of God governs every point on the spectrum of his life. This means then that when Baptists are simply exercising their beliefs such as preaching, planting churches, and calling people to a changed life, and opposition arises, the true Baptist believer will obey God's most perfect laws regardless of who else's laws this violates or whose feelings this hurts. So, when a Baptist revival broke out in the colonial, state-church era, it was inevitable that the Baptists would find themselves in political debate and turmoil almost immediately.

## The Age-Old Struggle For Liberty Of Conscience

Because of the persecution the Baptist people endured throughout Europe's history, the Lord's churches did not know of true liberty in any real sense. But, from the dark, damp torture chambers and burning stakes of Roman Catholicism, the early Baptist groups dreamed of the day when they could have their own public churches with their own pastors. Indeed, one of the untold stories of the Lord's churches throughout the Church Age is the hunger for liberty of conscience that God's people possessed. Baptists have always had a yearning for religious liberty.

Baptist Christianity started out in a position that made this longing for liberty a reality from the very beginning. The first Baptist, "John Baptist" (Luke 7:20), had his head cut off because he caused offense by speaking the Word of God. Jesus Christ was crucified on a cruel, Roman cross. The apostles are known to have suffered horrible tortures and deaths for identifying with Christ. In the early centuries imperial persecutions terrorized the primitive Baptist assemblies across Europe as men like Domitian, Diocletian, and Nero considered torturing God's people a fun activity, as if they were playing ball or going on an afternoon hunting trip with their children.

In AD 313 the Roman Catholic institution had its early foundation laid by the Roman emperor Constantine. Augustine of Hippo would then lay the heretical doctrinal foundation for this corrupt institution. The theology of Augustine became the framework for all of Catholic belief. This is often called dominion theology as it propagated the idea that the Roman Catholic institution is the kingdom of God on earth and must therefore march forward and gain new ground. Augustine laid out this idea in his book, *City of God*. Every sort of coercion, up to and including burning people alive and cutting their guts out, was practiced and justified within this corrupt system. Hence, on the heels of the creation of this murderous institution flung wide open the door to the Dark Ages.

For the next eleven hundred years the Lord's churches were massacred. From the dungeons of Rome, to the valleys of the Piedmont, to the burning stakes of England and beyond, the Christian groups that were slanderously called Ana-Baptists because of their demand for scriptural salvation and baptism were stoned, burned, disemboweled, decapitated, and literally mutilated and cut into bits by the millions!

When the great Protestant Reformation began, it did not take long for the Baptists to realize that there was largely no place of acceptance among the leading Reformers for them. Oliver Cromwell, although a political leader, became one of the only men of renown during the sixteenth and seventeenth centuries who was openly accepting of the Baptists. Sadly, this love affair dissolved quickly after Cromwell rose higher and became Lord Protector.

As Baptists began to migrate to America they were shocked and disappointed to see that things would be no different here. The state-sponsored churches were quickly set up in America and state-church colonial charters and laws written, signed and then ratified. The Baptists were disfranchised, and the quest for liberty carried on right up to the bitter end of the eighteenth century.

## The Baptists Gain Ground In Their Quest for Religious Liberty In America

At this time, it is necessary to introduce the incontrovertible spearhead in the Baptists' early movement toward entrenching religious liberty in America. His name is Dr. John Clarke. Clarke was among the first rays of liberty's light to shine within the boundaries of the future United States.

John Clarke was an English Baptist minister who sailed to America in 1637. Five of his siblings followed him to the New World. Clarke was truly a fascinating man. By the time Clarke landed in

America, he was not just acquainted with several fields of learning but literally mastered them all. He was first a master in theology and a decided Baptist. He caused the learned heathen of his day to stutter and second-guess themselves when he opened his mouth in defense of the Baptist faith. There were more than a few religious leaders and state officials who regretted undertaking a public debate with him. His skills in medicine were equally incredible; in fact, after his death he was honored for his medical contributions by the Newport Medical Society. Clarke also had a firm grasp on the principles of law. Clarke was not just the average lawyer. He focused his knowledge of the law toward the one area he was most well known for in the world- his expertise as a statesman and framer of civil government. When one considers just how brilliant a mind Clarke possessed and the many difficult fields he excelled in, one is dumb-founded. History struggles to produce an equal to the Baptist John Clarke.

Clarke landed in the New World in 1637; and there in Boston, he, along with his wife Elizabeth, began to minister to the needs of the people. Initially, his skill as a doctor was of utmost importance, as doctors were scarce and sickness was common in those days. However, it wasn't long before Clarke became a lightning rod of disruption and protest. Clarke very quickly became aware of the sad facts concerning the state-sponsored churches of New England. Roger Williams had been banished before Clarke ever arrived; and soon, the "magistrate's law" was passed. This law made it illegal to be affiliated with "non-approved" churches.

## Debate And Division

During this timeframe, there was debate in the air. The Antinomian debates involved the truths of law and grace. These debates began as discussions as to what evidence is accepted as proof of salvation. They evolved into full-blown bones of contention and ultimately into harsh division. The Antinomians were the preachers of grace and were within the bounds of sound theology in this particular debate. If a Congregational preacher were to embrace salvation without works, signs, or seals, he would be quickly banished or persuaded to continually embrace the errors of the establishment churches.

At this time, a woman named Anne Hutchison, an Antinomian, was ex-communicated from the state church. In March of 1638, the Reverend John Wilson, standing in his "crow's nest" pulpit, publicly stated these words:

> Therefore, in the name of the Lord Jesus Christ and in the name of the Church I do

> not only pronounce you worthy to be cast out, but I do cast you out; and in the name of Christ do I deliver you up to Satan, that you may learn no more to blaspheme, to seduce and to lie; and I do account you from this time forth to be a Heathen and a Publican, and so to be held of all the brethren and sisters of this congregation and of others; therefore, I command you in the name of Christ Jesus and of the church as a leper to withdraw yourself out of the congregation. [10]

In front of the Massachusetts Statehouse in Boston are two sobering statues. One is of Anne Hutchinson and the other is of Mary Dyer, a Quaker who was hung to death by the neck for her dissent from the colonial state-church. These two memorials are a small reminder of the many dissenters that were persecuted in New England in the Colonial Era. Hundreds were disfranchised, excommunicated, or met similar fates. Clarke himself was without a gun, as his weapons had been confiscated for suspicion of Anabaptism.

## The First Baptist Church

John Clarke knew that the time to leave was now. And the purpose for his leaving was to find

---

10 Wilbur Nelson, *The Hero of Aquidneck: A Life of Dr. John Clarke* (Grand Rapids: Fleming H. Revell, 1998), p. 25.

the religious liberty that the Baptists had desired for so long. He wanted a place to have a settled Baptist congregation. And with this in mind, he left Boston.

The first Baptist congregation in America existed in its infant form by the winter of 1637. Clarke's family and eighteen other families left Boston and first traveled northward to New Hampshire. This group despised the New Hampshire cold and could not find rest from religious persecution. These circumstances caused them to move. So in early 1638 they traveled southward into the Narragansett Bay. Here, freedom fighter Roger Williams coaxed them to move on to the island of Aquidneck. And this they did.

Before long, they landed on the island that would eventually be named Rhode Island. The year was 1638. They purchased this piece of land from the Indians and settled on its northern section. This little dot on a map, which they called Portsmouth, is where the famous *Portsmouth Compact*, authored by Clarke, was signed. The traveling group landed and immediately compacted together to form a government where religious persecution would not be tolerated. This truly was a landmark event.

Still in 1638, a portion of this original group, including Clarke, migrated to a little piece of ground on the south end of the island. They named the place Newport. Not only was Newport founded at this time, but it also became the permanent home for the first Baptist church on American soil. This church was not just the first Baptist church in Rhode Island, but was the first Baptist church in all of the colonies. This congregation, started and pastored at the first by Clarke, still exists today in Newport.

## Persecution In The Colonies Continued And Finally Hit Close To Home

While John Clarke was well acquainted with the oppression and outright persecution the Baptists had been experiencing at the hands of the establishment church officials, there was one specific event that took place that changed everything. This event would send shockwaves across the colonies and would eventually send Clarke sailing back across the ocean to spend a dozen years of his life in an attempt to win a charter honoring religious liberty for the Baptists and all the future inhabitants of Rhode Island.

## The Public Whipping Of The Baptist Obadiah Holmes

Obadiah Holmes was a member in good standing at the first Baptist church at Newport. In the summer of 1651, the Newport church received from the aged William Witter a request of visitation, so that he might hear the Word of God. Witter was also a member of the first Baptist church in Newport, Rhode Island. Being up in years now and blind, Witter was not able to travel to what was not only the nearest Baptist church, but what was one of the only organized Baptist churches on American soil. So upon Witter's request for a pastoral visit, Pastor John Clarke, church member John Crandall, and preacher Obadiah Holmes started out for Lynn, Massachusetts. They traveled eighty miles and arrived at Witter's home on Saturday night, July 19, 1651. They enjoyed a time of fellowship and prayer, and stayed at Witter's home that night, intending to worship together on the Lord's Day. News in Lynn spread fast and a warrant for the arrest of the strangers was delivered to the constable.

## A Stop At The State Church And A Trip To Boston

Holmes and company began their service the next morning; and after four or five visitors came, the constables burst in to break it up. The three men were taken into custody. That same day, the men were forced to attend an afternoon service in the Standing Order Congregational church. During the services Clarke attempted to preach and was silenced. Next, they were taken to prison.

On Tuesday, July 2, 1651, Holmes, Clarke, and Crandall were taken to Boston so that they might appear before their adversaries. They were committed to jail, and on July 31 they were tried in court. The Baptists were not presumed innocent but rather assumed guilty before the trial even started. After this mockery of a trial came the sentencing of the Baptists. The judge agreed with the prosecutor, Puritan preacher John Cotton, that this heresy of Anabaptism was worthy of death.

Holmes was fined thirty pounds or be "well whipt," Clarke was fined twenty pounds or to be "well whipt," and Crandall five pounds or to be "well whipt." Money was raised to pay the fines. Crandall was released from his fine. Clarke and Holmes refused permission for their fines to be paid, not willing to admit guilt, yet knowing the dreaded whipping post was the alternative.

## The Whipping Of Holmes

As Clarke was led to the whipping post, a friend pressed money into the hands of the Puritan official accompanying the party, and Clarke was released. But Holmes believed that yielding to state church tyranny by paying his fine would have been equivalent to admitting wrongdoing. Holmes was led to the post and stripped to the waist. While being stripped, Obadiah Holmes preached a sermon to the on-looking crowd, exhorting them to stay faithful to their beliefs. Obadiah Holmes's sentence was ten stripes less than the maximum of forty lashes, which was considered a death sentence and was the same sentence as was imposed upon rapists. Many in the gathering crowd cried out in protest. At least thirteen individuals were arrested for calling for the punishment to stop, as the beating was an attempt to kill Holmes.

Holmes was beaten on the Boston Square, which was the same place the famed Boston Massacre would take place over one hundred years later. Both events exemplify a struggle for different aspects of the same principle-liberty. Holmes was beaten for religious liberty, whereas, the Boston Massacre took place over political liberty.

Holmes stated that the flogger used a whip with three hard leather lashes and gave this account of his beating:

> And as the man began to lay the strokes upon my back, I said to the people, though my flesh should fail, and my spirit should fail, yet God would not fail; so it pleased the Lord to come in, and to fill my heart and tongue as a vessel full; and with an audible voice I break forth crying the Lord not to lay this sin to their charge, and telling the people that now I found he did not fail me,

> and therefore now I should trust him forever who failed me not; for in truth, as the strokes fell upon me, I had such a spiritual manifestation of God's presence, as I never had before, and the outward pain was so removed from me, that I could well bear it, yea, and in a manner felt it not, although it was grievous, as the spectators said, the man striking with all his strength, spitting in his hand three times, with a three corded whip, giving me therewith thirty strokes.[11]

The unbroken spirit of Holmes and the Baptists of New England was exemplified in the statement Holmes made to the magistrates as he was released from the post. He boldly stated, **"You have struck me as with roses."**[12] This cruel beating did not stop the Baptists, but rather emboldened them.

Dr. John Clarke, following the beating of Holmes, wrote *Ill Newes from New England* (1652). In it, Dr. Clarke presented his philosophy of government. He pushed for the government not to interfere with man's conscience on religious matters. Soon after, it was decided that Roger Williams and John Clarke would sail for England to persuade the King to grant Rhode Island a charter of full religious liberty. The people raised the money to sponsor Clarke who

---

11 Isaac Backus, *History of New England*, Vol. 1 (Paris: The Baptist Standard Bearer, 1871, reprinted), p. 192.
12 Ibid

would stay in England long after Williams returned to America. Clarke wrote up a charter to present to King Charles II. After twelve long years, and by some strange miracle, the king granted Clarke the stamp of approval, and Rhode Island was established upon the principles of a charter hand-written by the Baptist preacher.

## The Amazing Rhode Island Charter

In the Rhode Island State House in Providence, framed in an impressive fire-proof, climate controlled safe in its own individual museum, is housed one of the most uniquely important documents ever produced in the history of the world. This document granted "a full liberty in religious concernments" to the people of Rhode Island. The *Rhode Island Charter*, sometimes referred to as the *Colonial Charter of 1663*, was authored and won virtually single-handedly by none other than Dr. John Clarke. This ancient document, beautifully penned on fine parchment, should be studied, modeled, and appreciated by individuals and governments throughout the world. Carved into the marble above the south entrance of the Providence State House are the following words taken from the charter itself:

"To–Hold–Forth–A–Lively–Experiment–

# LAID BY THE BAPTISTS 49

That–A–Most–Flourishing–Civil–State–May–Stand–And–Best–Be–Maintained–With–Full–Liberty–In–Religious–Concernments."

The previous principles are what Clarke called, "a lively experiment."

By the time 1663 rolled around, Clarke had spent a total of thirteen years as an ambassador sent from Rhode Island. His sole purpose was to persuade the Crown, through much diplomacy and scholarly evidence, that there was a great need for liberty of conscience in the New World.

As has been mentioned, in 1652, Clarke wrote his famous book entitled *Ill Newes from New England*. In this book he proclaimed the mistreatment of the Baptist brethren in the New World. One popular statement in this book reads as such: "While Old England is becoming new, New England is becoming old."[13] This burden he carried and this burden he pled until Charles II granted him the charter in 1663.

## The Immediate Impact Of The Colonial Charter On The Colonies

This one document immediately established Rhode Island as the freest city-state in the known world! It granted to its citizens full religious liberty.

---

13 John Clarke, *Ill Newes from New England*, (London: Henry Hills, 1652).

Finally, liberty had started to break through in the American colonies; and the Baptists were not just leading the charge, they were the charge!

## The Lasting Impact Of The Colonial Charter On America And The World

There are two key areas in which this Baptist work would become foundational to all of America.

*Firstly, The Early Colonial Charter, Which Was Rhode Island's Founding Document, Was Clearly A Primary Blueprint For Our Nation's Founding Documents.*

The Charter itself was so masterfully crafted, that the citizens of Rhode Island used it as their ruling document for nearly two centuries. This charter was the ruling document in Rhode Island until the colony became a state, and then it became the state constitution for another sixty-seven years. The present-day state constitution was adopted in 1843 and holds much of the same principles the original charter did. The original colonial charter was then retired. For one hundred eighty years, this Baptist-penned document governed the state of Rhode Island and Providence Plantations.

Thomas Jefferson is said to have given Dr. John Clarke the credit for obtaining this remarkable charter and to have named it as one of the sources from which he derived the principles of the Declaration of Independence.[14]

In addition, since this document above all others held the most forceful stand for individualistic religious liberty of any other early colonial document, it was the one perfect example to the founding fathers that a religious liberty amendment to the U.S. Constitution was not only plausible but imperative! The charter was proven to have stood the test of time as morally right and beneficial in every way. It honored the autonomy of the individual, while knitting together a corporate people in a free and prosperous governmental arrangement.

The Baptist preacher John Clarke understood principles of civil government and religious liberty much more clearly than any other man in the early colonial timeframe, saving for Roger Williams, who was closely related to the Baptists in thought and theory. But even Williams did not surpass Clarke. Case in point: Clarke penned the charter, while Williams did not!

The principles in the Rhode Island Charter made their way into our founding documents, and therefore American principles of civil government are partly, if not largely, Baptist principles of civil government.

---

14 Nelson, 62.

*The Second Way This Charter Had Lasting Effects: Not Only Did The Charter Become A Blueprint For The Framers To Study And Consider As They Drafted Our Founding Documents, But The Colony Of Rhode Island Itself Became The Example Of What A Land Of Liberty Looked Like.*

It is no coincidence that the United States is founded on the principle of individual liberty as Rhode Island was. The American "Idea" was simply a "Borrowed Idea." And it was borrowed from the Baptists. The First Amendment holds the same principle that John Clarke wrote into the Charter! Had the model for America been that of Virginia, Massachusetts, or North Carolina, which were all state-church hotbeds, persecution and public whippings may still exist today. Every American who loves to freely think and/or worship should be thankful that the established framework of America closely mirrors that of the Baptist colony of Rhode Island.

The questions must be asked then, what model would America resemble if Clarke hadn't made sure Rhode Island was as it was? What documents would have filled the vacuum if the Charter of 1663 was not written and won through thirteen years of labor by Clarke? The framers certainly would have had one less sound source from which to consult and borrow principles.

If it were possible to subtract John Clarke and

the New England Baptists from the equation that ultimately equals America, God only knows what the impact of such a devastating subtraction would be!

## There Is A Second Major Phase Of Influence That The Baptists Inserted Into The Base Layer Of America's Political Foundations.

While there are many ways in which the Baptists contributed in a positive fashion from the time of the birth of Rhode Island until the 1760s, the biggest political impact they would have would begin to unfold just prior to beginning of the Revolution.

At the beginning of this chapter, the author stated, "In this study of Baptist influences on America, one does not have to shift too many gears when moving his thought pattern from the spiritual contributions of the Baptists to their political contributions." Now this statement will be further explained.

The largest spiritual influence of the Baptists on America started at Sandy Creek, North Carolina. This revival would send men all directions preaching the Gospel. The most powerful arm of this revival burst northward into Virginia where the flood tide of Baptists would have a marked effect on this established Anglican colony. The many Baptist transplants as well as the new converts to the Baptist faith would set the stage for the next phase in the Baptist battle to establish religious liberty.

Whereas Shubal Stearns and Daniel Marshall were the clear leaders of the Separate Baptist Revival in North Carolina and southward, a man named Colonel Samuel Harriss became one of the great spiritual leaders among the Separate Baptists in Virginia.

Harriss was born in Virginia on January 12, 1724. He grew into a man of accomplishment. He became the Church Warden, justice of the peace, sheriff, burgess of the county, colonel of the militia, captain of Fort Mayo, and commissary for the fort and the army.

Dan River, a Separate Baptist congregation in southern Virginia, was organized in 1760. Before long, Dan River began to spread its branches, and five other works were begun by 1772. As the Baptists of this area preached in the surrounding region, many were saved. One such man was Colonel Samuel Harriss whose glorious conversion is recorded for us by the historian Cathcart:

> It is said that when engaged in the army, in the discharge of his official duties, he providentially found an opportunity of hearing the gospel by Joseph and William Murphy, who had appointed a meeting at a house near Allen's Creek, on the road leading

from Booker's Ferry, on Staunton, to Pittsylvania Court-house. As the people were collecting, Colonel Harriss rode up, splendidly attired in his military habit. "What is to be done here, gentlemen?" said Harriss. "Preaching, Colonel." "Who is to preach?" "The Murphy boys, sir." "I believe I will stop and hear them." He dismounted. The house was small, and in one corner stood a loom, behind which the colonel seated himself. The Lord's eye was upon him, and the truth became effectual in deepening his convictions. Such was his agony of mind that at the close of the meeting his sword and other parts of his regimentals were found scattered around him. His conversion was brought to pass in an unusual manner; it began with a deep seriousness without his knowing why or wherefore; conversation and reading, directed his attention to the cause; pressed with this conviction he ventured to attend the ministry of the Baptists; his distress increased; and his heart was ready to burst. Once as the people rose from prayer, the Colonel was observed to continue on his knees, with his head and his hands hanging down the other side of the bench; some of the people went to his relief, and found he was senseless as in a fit; when he came to himself he smiled, and brake out in an ecstasy of joy, crying, "Glory! Glory! Glory!"[15]

---

15 William Cathcart, p. 504.

Harriss's conversion took place in 1758 at thirty-four years of age. Harriss was baptized at the hands of Daniel Marshall into the membership of the Dan River Baptist Church. Before long, the call of God upon Harriss's life became evident. By 1759, Harriss was preaching with all authority. Sprague recorded the following concerning Harriss, "When he first began to preach, his soul was so absorbed in the work, that it was difficult for him to attend to duties of this life."[16]

Harriss was ordained and began to minister mostly in Pittsylvania and the surrounding counties. On October 11, 1769, he was ordained as an evangelist. The first man baptized at his hands was the famed James Ireland. Ireland would become a tremendous preacher, and his imprisonments in Culpeper are famous among Baptist historians. Ireland related the following narrative concerning Harriss's ordination:

> I saw him ordained and a moving time it was. He was considered a great man in the things of time and sense; but he shone more conspicuously in the horizon of the church, during the time of our sweet intercourse together, so that he was like another Paul among the churches. No man like-minded with him, who like a blazing comet, would

---
16 William Buell Sprague, *Annals of the American Pulpit: Baptists,* (New York: Robert Carter and Brothers, 1860), p. 81.

rush through the colony or state displaying the banners of his adorable Master, spreading His light and diffusing His heat to the consolation of thousands.[17]

## HOLY, ANOINTED PREACHING

Having an unusual anointing of God on his preaching, and a presence that commanded respect, Harriss was used greatly in southern Virginia. His preaching was with heavenly, angelic fire. The Virginia Baptist historian Semple stated that-

> "His excellency lay chiefly in addressing the heart; and perhaps even Whitfield [sic] did not surpass him in this respect. When animated himself, he seldom failed to animate his auditory. Some have described him, when exhorting at great meetings, as pouring forth streams of celestial lightning from his eyes; which, whithersoever he turned his face, would strike down hundreds at once."[18]

## Harriss Heads To Northern Virginia Where His Preaching Is Blessed Of Heaven In Spite Of His Being Surrounded By Persecution

---

17 Lewis Peyton Little, *Imprisoned Preachers and Religious Liberty in Virginia* (Lynchburg: J. P. Bell Co.), p. 151.
18 Robert Baylor Semple, *A History of the Rise and Progress of the Baptists in Virginia* (Richmond: published by the author, printed by John O'Lynch, 1810), p. 379.

The timeframe in which Harriss began his itinerant evangelistic ministry was during a period of religious persecution in Virginia. Cathcart's record of the persecution is as follows:

> For three or four years there had been severe persecutions of the Baptists in many parts of Virginia. Letters were received at this association from preachers confined in prison, particularly from David Tinsley, then in Chesterfield jail. The hearts of their brethren were affected at their sufferings, in consequence of which it was agreed to raise contributions for their aid. The following resolution was entered into: Agreed to set apart the second and third Saturdays in June as public fast days, in behalf of our poor blind persecutors, and for the releasement of our brethren.[19]

At least forty-five Baptist ministers sat in prisons during this timeframe for simply preaching the gospel. Harriss was hated by the established church of Virginia as evidenced in the following narrative of his first preaching tour in the northern part of Virginia:

> Arriving in Culpeper, his first meeting was at Wyley's own house. He preached the first day without interruption, and appointed for

---
19 Ibid, p. 56

> the next. He the next day began to preach, but the opposers immediately raised violent opposition, appearing with whip, sticks, clubs, &c. so as to hinder his labours; in consequence of which he went that night over to Orange county, and preached with much effect. He continued many days preaching from place to place, attended by great crowds, and followed throughout his meetings by several persons who had been either lately converted, or seriously awakened, under the ministry of the Regular Baptists, and also by many who had been alarmed by his own labours.[20]

On another occasion, Harriss was arrested and carried into court on charges as a disturber of the peace. In court, a captain Williams vehemently accused him of being a vagabond, a heretic, and a mover of sedition everywhere. Mr. Harriss made his defense, but the court ordered that he should not preach in the county again for the space of twelve months or be committed to prison. The colonel responded to the court that he lived two hundred miles from thence and that it was not likely that he should disturb them again in the course of one year. Upon this remark, he was dismissed. From Culpeper, he went into Fauquier and preached at Carter's Run. From thence he crossed the Blue Ridge

---
20 Ibid, p. 20

and preached in Shenandoah.

The persecution followed Harriss into Orange County as one man named Healey pulled Harriss down as he was preaching and dragged him about, sometimes by the hair of the head and sometimes by the leg, finally being rescued by his friends. In another instance, Harriss was knocked down by a rude fellow while he was preaching. Once he went to preach to the prisoners in the town of Hillsborough. The response by the constables was to lock him in and keep him there for some time.

In spite of all the opposition, his ministry was nearly unbelievable! Souls were saved, men were called to preach and sent out, and churches were planted. These events happened so often, on such a large scale, and over such a vast region that it is truly impossible to ascertain everything God accomplished through Samuel Harriss. It is widely believed that Harriss had a direct part in birthing over sixty churches. As all this activity went on, the Anglican colony of Virginia was steadily being transformed into a Baptist revival grounds!

**Orange And Culpeper**

Harriss began making tours through north central and eastern Virginia in 1765, which he would do repeatedly for many years. On the first tour, Semple stated that Harriss preached often and "sowed many

# LAID BY THE BAPTISTS  61

good seed, yielding afterwards great increase."[21] Harriss left young converts in Orange and Culpeper, Virginia. After Harriss's departure, these converts became discouraged by David Thomas, a staunch Calvinistic Baptist minister who was a Regular Baptist from the Philadelphia Association. Thomas squelched the zeal of the young converts and their thoughts of preaching without formal training. After this, they beckoned Harriss again. In 1766, Harriss returned to the area along with the Separate Baptist James Read. In Orange, they baptized nineteen on the first day and many more on the days that followed. Semple records that, "On one of their visits they baptized seventy-five at one time, and in the course of one of their journeys, which generally lasted several weeks, they baptized upwards of two hundred."[22] Harriss and Read proceeded to preach in Spotsylvania, Upper Caroline, Hanover, and Goochland counties. Such was their success that they determined to return the next year to do the same. This they did, accompanied by the Separate Baptist preacher Dutton Lane.

## Enter John Leland

Samuel Harriss's preaching in north central Virginia, combined with all the persecutions and im-

---

21  Ibid, p. 21
22  Ibid, p. 23

prisonments, became the unfolding backdrop of the greatest political contribution to America that Baptists have ever made. The contribution was the establishment of full liberty of conscience.

Although many Baptists took their stand in the battle for religious freedom and some even suffered great loss, one man rose to the pinnacle and became the mind, pen, voice, diplomat, statesman, and warrior for the Baptists. That man was Elder John Leland. Leland would become a key author, along with Baptist minister Reuben Ford, of the many petitions the Baptists circulated. These petitions calling for complete religious liberty were submitted to the Virginia legislature on many occasions. One of these petitions was so large and held so many signatures that it had to be delivered in a wheelbarrow. The results of these petitions, coupled with the Baptists' willingness to sit in prison for conscience sake, were many. Butterfield explains: "The Baptists had resorted to political action in their own behalf soon after they gained enough strength to become organized."[23] He continued by saying, "...the political drift of the times greatly favored the dissenters...in Virginia, Mason, Jefferson, and Madison [all friends of liberty]...were determined to do

---

23 Lyman H. Butterfield, *Elder John Leland, Jeffersonian Itinerant* (Worcester: American Antiquarian Society, 1952), p.173

something about it."[24]

The first reward of the political action of the Baptists was in the form of the Declaration of Rights of 1776. This prefix to the Virginia Constitution contained the following words: "... all men should enjoy the fullest toleration in the exercise of religion according to the dictates of conscience."[25] James Madison petitioned and successfully had these words changed to read, "... are equally entitled to the free exercise of religion."[26] This slight change was of the utmost importance since toleration implies a favor granted, whereas free exercise recognizes an existing inalienable right.

Although the Baptists were pleased with this accomplishment, it did not, however, abolish the state-sponsored churches within Virginia. The Baptists continued to push to this end. "A flood of petitions deluged the legislature... [as Baptists insisted that] this house will go on to complete what is so nobly begun, by abolishing all church establishments in Virginia."[27] Over the next ten years the Baptists continued to petition for a complete separation of church and state. The Baptists gained another civil victory when in 1779 tithes to the establishment church were abolished.

---

24 Ibid, p.173
25 Ibid, p.173
26 Virginia Declaration of Rights (June 12, 1776), Article XVI
27 Butterfield, 174

In 1781, Thomas Jefferson retired from Virginia politics and James Madison was thrust to the forefront of the battle for separation of church and state. His first accomplishment, rephrasing George Mason's wording in the Virginia Bill of Rights, has been previously discussed. Madison's next accomplishment toward liberty was in 1785 when he introduced Thomas Jefferson's bill for religious freedom. In 1786, it passed to the rejoicing of the Baptists.

About this time, John Leland became a great force, relentlessly fighting for a complete separation of the state and church. In 1786 the Baptist general committee backed Leland and Reuben Ford in an effort to repeal an act that incorporated the Episcopal Church. At this time, the Episcopal Church still held lands that were granted to it while under the old establishment arrangement. This act was a desperate attempt to hold on to these valuable properties. The Baptists and their petitions were successful, and the act was repealed.

The condition of the Virginia Baptists concerning liberty was greatly improving. They were no longer looked upon with widespread disdain as they had been before Leland arrived in Virginia. There was, however, one more war for Leland to wage. This would prove to be the most important civil duty Leland would perform.

## John Leland, James Madison, And The Federal Bill Of Rights

When the Constitution was written and submitted to the states for consideration, John Leland's critical eye noticed a key provision was excluded. The provision he was looking for was a statement that would ingrain the principles of religious liberty and separation of church and state onto the mantle of the new nation. The Constitution, however, only contained one reference to religion and that being the prohibition of religious tests as qualifications for federal offices. Although Article VI is a great inclusion, it wasn't enough for Mr. Leland! The Baptist general committee agreed with Leland that the Constitution was not sufficient without a declaration of full religious liberty.

At this time, all eyes were on Virginia. The state was by "position, size, and prestige...delicately balanced between approval and disapproval."[28] James Madison was in New York writing the "Federalist" papers when he received a letter from his father. James Madison, Sr., wrote the following on January 30th, 1788: "The Baptists are now generally opposed to it [the Constitution]."[29] Then on February 17th, James Gordon, Jr., a candidate for the Constitutional Congress himself, wrote to Madison

---
28  Ibid, p. 183
29  Ibid, p.184

and said, "...I think it is incumbent on you without delay, to repair to this state, as the loss of the Constitution in this state may involve consequences the most alarming to every citizen of America."[30]

At this time, Madison decided to run for a seat at the Ratifying Convention and left for Virginia. While in Fredericksburg, he received yet another letter which alarmed him. This letter was written by Captain Joseph Spencer, a Baptist who had at one time been persecuted and imprisoned in Virginia, and read, "The...Constitution has its enemies in Orange...The preachers of that Society are much alarmed fearing religious liberty is not sufficiently secured...Mr. Leland, and Mr. Bledsoe, and Sanders are the most public men of the society in Orange, therefore as Mr. Leland lies in your way home from Fredericksburg to Orange would advise you'd call on him and spend a few hours in his company...The enclosure is a copy of 'objections' to the Constitution set down by John Leland..."[31] (all three letters are from the Madison Papers, Library of Congress). The tenth objection in the list of Leland's objections to the Constitution reads as follows:

> "What is clearest of all-Religious Liberty, is not sufficiently secured, .No Religious test is Required as a qualification to fill any office

---

30 Ibid, p.185
31 Ibid, p.186

under the United States, but if a Majority of Congress with the President favour one System more then another, they may oblige all others to pay to the support of their System as much as they please, and if Oppression does not ensue, it will be owing to the Mildness of Administration and not to any Constitutional defence, and if the Manners of People are so far Corrupted, that they cannot live by Republican principles, it is Very Dangerous leaving Religious Liberty at their Mercy."[32]

## The Meeting That Changed The Course Of America And Won The Age-Old Battle For Liberty Of Conscience

Madison, who was concerned not only with his own political future as a candidate to Virginia's Ratifying Convention but also with the future of America, met with Leland to discuss Leland's objections. After Leland was assured that Madison would, if given a chance, present a bill of rights guaranteeing full religious liberty at a later date, Leland agreed to support Madison's election. An account of this meeting "appears in the standard town history of Cheshire, Massachusetts."[33] In another form this meeting was published in *Harper's* monthly magazine in 1881 as such, "In pronouncing a eulogy at

---
32 Ibid, p.188
33 Ibid, p. 189

Culpeper Courthouse in July, 1836, John Strode Barbour discussed at some length the close alliance between Madison and the Baptists and said that his election to the Virginia Ratifying Convention… was owing to his changing the minds of two Baptist ministers on the eve of the election…John Leland was one of them."[34]

With Madison's promise secured, Leland persuaded the Baptists to vote for Madison. Madison beat his nearest opponent [Gordon] by 15 votes. Then in June, Virginia ratified the Constitution by a vote of 89 to 79.

Keep in mind that if Samuel Harriss and other preachers had not flooded Orange and Culpeper counties with their multitudes of Baptist converts, Leland would not have had the leverage he needed to persuade Madison of the absolute necessity of an established right of individual religious liberty.

The author firmly believes that the obedience of the Separate Baptists, to preach the Word of God contrary to state-church law and endure many hardships, may have caused the Lord to bless them with religious liberty.

## Madison Keeps His Promise To The Baptists Of Virginia

The following year, with the full vote of the

---
[34] Ibid, p. 190

Baptists, Madison handed James Monroe a crushing defeat and was elected to the first Congress of the United States of America. Leland wrote Madison a personal congratulatory letter. It said among other things, "One thing I shall expect; that if religious liberty is anywise threatened, that I shall receive the earliest intelligence."[35] This letter gives clear proof of their friendship as it ends with these words: "I take the liberty of writing this to you, lest I should not be at home when you pass by on your way to Congress."[36]

Madison wasted no time on the floor of Con-

---

35 Leland, in a letter from the undated *Madison Papers*, cited by Butterfield in ibid, p. 194.

36 Ibid

\* (From the Author) The reader, upon a quick perusal, will notice a series of quotations from L.H. Butterfield. These quotes are many, but are vital to a book such as this. Butterfield is considered by many to be the one true Leland biographer. His credentials speak for themselves.

"Lyman Henry Butterfield served as an associate editor of the first five volumes of The Papers of Thomas Jefferson (published by Princeton University Press) and then as Director of the Institute of Early American History and Culture at Williamsburg; from 1954 to 1975 he served as editor-in-chief of the Adams Papers, and under his active editorship or editorial direction appeared the first twenty volumes of [t]his monumental project, conducted with the cooperation of the Adams family, the sponsorship of the Massachusetts Historical Society, and the imprint of the Belknap Press of Harvard University Press."

Previous information from: Mark S. Scarberry, Professor of Law, Pepperdine University School of Law. John Leland and James Madison: Religious Influence on the Ratification of the Constitution and on the Proposal of the Bill of Rights. (borrowed from p. 734 PENN STATE LAW REVIEW [Vol. 113:3])

gress introducing a series of amendments, which would become known as The Bill of Rights. The first of these says, "Congress shall make no law respecting the establishment of religion, or prohibiting the free exercise thereof." Historian Robert Dalton stated, "The crowning, if not permanent victory, was won in America in 1791 with the passage of the First Amendment."[37]

Every citizen of this great country has tremendously benefited from these grand principles. What most people don't know is that if there never was a meeting between John Leland and James Madison, America may not have ratified the Constitution. In addition to this, the rights and liberties we take for granted would not have been a reality. Truly, America could be a very different place!

Joseph Dawson in *Baptists and the American Republic* said, "The first amendment was the fulfillment by Madison of a promise made to the Baptist evangelist John Leland and the Baptists in Virginia."[38]

The following picture shows the author at the Leland / Madison Park in Orange, VA. This park and monument commemorate the historic meeting between the two men.

---

[37] Robert Dalton, *Struggle for Liberty: The Baptists, The Bible and Church-State Conflict in Colonial America* (Bloomington: Author House, 2004), p. 84.

[38] Joseph Martin Dawson, *Baptists and the American Republic* (New York: Arno Press, 1980), pp. 115-116.

# LAID BY THE BAPTISTS

William Estep related, "Butterfield examines the evidence for and against the alleged meeting of Leland and Madison at Gum Springs (now the Leland-Madison Park) and concludes that the circumstantial evidence suggesting such a meeting is very strong, as is the local tradition, which was very much alive at the time of Madison's death in 1836. Butterfield writes, 'There can be no question that the monument [at the park] memorializes an actual occurrence.'"[39]

---

[39] William Roscoe Estep, *Revolution Within the Revolution: The First Amendment in Historical Context, 1612-1789* (Grand Rapids: Wm. B. Eerdmans Publishing Co., 1990) pp. 156-179.

## Tying It Together

When one considers the Portsmouth Compact, the Rhode Island Charter of 1663, the Rhode Island Model, the willingness of at least forty-five Baptist preachers to sit in prison as they demanded religious liberty, and the petitions, the counsel, leadership and efforts of John Leland and many others, it becomes as clear as crystal: that without the Baptists, America may not have the religious liberty that every American citizen enjoys to this very day! Truly the series of victories that the Virginia Baptists had won in their colonial government were the precursor to the victory the Baptists later won for the other twelve colonies! If the reader appreciates his religious liberty he is hereby encouraged to thank God for the colonial Baptists.

# 3. The Foundations Of The American Revolution Were Laid By The Baptists

In the mid-1760s, as the Separate Baptist Revival was in full swing in North Carolina and true religion was flourishing, something else was brewing in North Carolina. Unforeseen by many Baptists at the time, the American Revolution was just around the bend.

The influence of the Revolutionary War on the colonies is a well-known and common narrative in American history books. But, sadly, the influence of the Baptists on the Revolution and on its victorious outcome is almost completely unknown to the world.

Baptist historian William Cathcart said it best in the preface of *Baptist Patriots and the American Revolution:*

> Baptists have ever been the ardent friends of civil and religious liberty. Their history in the New World overflows with testimonies of this character. They have never regarded the military profession with much favor and, as a rule, have only resorted to

arms in great emergencies when the worst evils threatened an entire people. So that we must not look for them among the principal commanders of the Revolution. The leading men of Massachusetts and Virginia, the two great arms of the Revolution, were hostile to the Baptists, and had lent their aid to laws which grievously persecuted them right down to the commencement of the great struggle, and it is not to be expected that they would place members of the "Sect everywhere spoken against" in prominent military positions... Notwithstanding these considerations our brethren acted a glorious part in the conflict, which secured our liberties, and which set the world an example which so many nations have already followed.[40]

## Prelude To The Revolution

The American Revolutionary War was not brought on in a day. The fires of revolution were slowly kindled throughout the colonies. In no place was this truer than in the province of North Carolina.

*Sugar Act*

As early as 1764, public outrage at the British Parliament's tax policy was expressed in North Car-

---

40 William Cathcart, *The Baptists and the American Revolution* (Lansing: Calvary Publishing, reprint, 1876), pp. 3-4, Preface.

olina. On October 31 of this same year, anger over the Sugar Act was proclaimed as North Carolina legislators denounced the new tax policy.

*Stamp Act*

In March of 1765, Parliament passed the infamous Stamp Act. Under this act, bills of lading, legal documents, pamphlets, newspapers, and numerous other items were required to carry stamps. On October 19, 1765, over five hundred people in the lower Cape Fear area of North Carolina converged near Wilmington. They demonstrated with a bonfire and mock hanging of Lord Bute. Some historians believe that the "Sons of Liberty" were born on this night. The Sons of Liberty would become a zealous group of patriots who opposed the king and Parliament's taxes and encroachment.

*Townshend Act*

Parliament passed the Townsend Act in 1767. Duties were placed on imported wine, paper, lead, glass, and tea. On November 11, 1768, the General Assembly of North Carolina offered an address to the king. Speaker of the House John Harvey said, "Free men cannot legally be taxed but by themselves or their representative..."[41]

On November 2, 1769, Speaker Harvey presented the Virginia resolutions of non-importation to the North Carolina legislature. When the lower house adopted these resolutions, the governor dissolved the assembly. This would prove to be the straw that would break the camel's back.

*Governor Tryon, An Enemy*

William Tryon became governor of North Carolina in May of 1765. From the beginning of his governorship he proved to be an enemy of liberty, self-rule, and the Baptist people. Tryon had a corrupt group of subordinates under his leadership. Baptist historian William Lumpkin said of Tryon's crew of corrupt politicians that they "pocketed over half of the tax money they collected."[42] He went on to say that the "officials scorned the poor and took advantage of the ignorant."[43] Sheriffs' embezzlements in 1767 alone amounted to $200,000.[44]

In addition to the corrupt tax collectors, the Provincial Assembly in North Carolina was controlled by wealthy plantation owners from the East where

---

41 Jeffrey J. Crow, *A Chronicle of North Carolina During the American Revolution 1768-1789* (Raleigh: North Carolina Division of Archives and History, 1975), p. 9.
42 Lumpkin, p. 74
43 Ibid
44 *North Carolina Baptist Historical Papers, II* (April, 1898), pp. 137.

Tryon lived. Thus, the average North Carolinian was misrepresented or not represented at all.

*Governor Tryon Hated Baptists*
In 1766 Tryon passed a marriage act that put Baptists and other dissenters on the wrong side of the law if they performed weddings. According to the historian Paschal, Tryon called the Baptists "enemies to society and a scandal to common sense."[45]

*The Regulators*
As a result of all the corruption, the mistreatment of the Baptists and other dissenting groups, lack of representation, and exorbitant taxes, the Baptists would make history by leading in a pre-Revolutionary War liberty movement. These liberty lovers would become known as the "Regulation." The Regulators were largely Baptist groups that stepped to the forefront in opposing Governor Tryon and his corrupt and oppressive government. Benjamin Merrill was a key leader of this movement. Captain Merrill was a member of the Jersey Settlement Baptist Church where John Gano pastored.

*The Battle Of Alamance*
On May 16, 1771, Governor Tryon and his army met the Regulators on a piece of ground near Ala-

---
45 Lumpkin, p. 76.

mance Creek. In less than two hours, Tryon's force decimated the Regulators. This defeat quenched the immediate fire. But as the sparks flew upward, these sparks would become a great, unquenchable flame called the Revolution.

## The Effects Of The Battle Of Alamance And Governor Tryon On The Baptists

*1. Captain Merrill And Five Others Were Hanged In Hillsborough*

South of Lexington, not far from the Jersey Baptist Church, Benjamin Merrill's plantation was overrun and he was arrested. Chief Justice Howard pronounced the following sentence:

> "...that you, Benjamin Merrill, be carried to the place from whence you came; that you be drawn from thence to the place of execution, where you are to be hanged by the neck; that you be cut down while yet alive; that your bowels be taken out while you are yet alive and burnt before your face; that your head be cut off, and your body divided into four quarters, and this to be at his Majesty's disposal; and the Lord have mercy on your soul."[46]

*2. The North Carolina Baptists Decimated And*

---

46 Garland A. Hendricks, *Saints and Sinners* (Thomasville: Charity and Children, 1964) p. 22.

## LAID BY THE BAPTISTS

*Driven Away*

Governor Tryon and his militia knew the Regulators were mostly Baptists, so he attacked and drove away the Baptists at Sandy Creek, Abbott's Creek, Shallow Fords, Deep Creek, Belew's Creek, Hunting Creek, and Jersey Settlement. He wasted their plantations and apprehended many, putting them into prison.

In *Baptist Foundations in the South*, we read the following: "The Sandy Creek folk, nevertheless, knew a week of terror during the encampment of the army, whose intentions could only be guessed. The week was sufficient to convince most members of Sandy Creek Church that they must migrate."[47]

Although Sandy Creek was reduced to less than twenty members at this time, the churches and ministers that she produced would not be stopped. Sandy Creek Church had already flung her seeds, and the crop was blooming in all directions. At this time the greatest area of Separate Baptist Revival activity would become Virginia.

According to Morgan Edwards around fifteen hundred families left North Carolina following Alamance.

---

[47] Lumpkin, p. 83.

## The Baptist Regulators Paved The Way For The American Revolution

Garland A. Hendricks stated in his book *Saints and Sinners*, "The kind of defeat which they suffered most certainly made some of the survivors more determined than ever to stand firm upon the principles of freedom and of separation of church and state."[48] The truth of this quote would be evidenced in Virginia, Tennessee, Kentucky, and everywhere else the Separate Baptists would migrate. The Baptists were the early backbone of a much larger contingency of colonists who were now cocked back on their haunches and ready to fight for liberty.

The Baptists were not idle during the Revolution. That the Revolution was used by God to produce a nation that would bless the Jew, spread the Gospel, and publish the Word of God is indisputable; that He used His people, the Baptists, to accomplish these ends is also a glaring fact of history.

## Key Thesis On How The North Carolina Baptists Challenged And Strengthened The Other Colonies To Stand Up To An Oppressive And Unreasonable English King

Truly, the first battles of the Revolution may have been Lexington and Concord, but it was a

---
48 Hendricks, p. 25.

North Carolina skirmish that inspired the various colonies to ultimately take up arms to fight a full-fledged Revolution. Yet remember- the Baptists were single handedly fighting their own revolution before 1772! When nearly no one else was fighting England's tyranny, the liberty loving Baptists were.

Historian William Cathcart puts forth an interesting thesis in his great book *Baptist Patriots and the American Revolution*. Cathcart teaches that the non-Baptist colonists actually learned how to resist tyranny and stand for liberty from the often, persecuted Baptists. The principles that the whole would embrace and fight for were simply the principles the Baptists for decades had fought for by themselves. Consider the following points as evidence of this idea.

## Baptists Demanded Liberty Long Before The Revolution

They were fined, beaten, banished, and disfranchised repeatedly by oppressive colonial governments and yet protested and endured without wavering.

## The Baptists Supported The Continental Congress.

The first Continental Congress assembled on September 5, 1774. The Baptists were among the earliest religions to support it. The New England Baptists of the Warren Association, eight days after the origination of the Continental Congress, declared it the supreme court of the American colonies and said that they were "...willing to unite with our dear countrymen to pursue every prudent measure for relief."[49] The Philadelphia Baptist Association supported the Continental Congress as well.

## The Baptists Took Their Place On The Battlefields.

The Virginian historian Howison stated, "No class of the people of America were more devoted advocates of the principles of the Revolution, none were more willing to give their money and goods to their country, none more prompt to march to the field of battle, and none more heroic in actual conflict than the Baptists of Virginia."[50]

## Baptist Chaplains

Baptist preachers from numerous locations were zealous in their desire to serve as chaplains. John Gano, Hezekiah Smith, and Charles Thompson, to name a few, served faithfully in this capacity. George Washington once stated, "Baptist chaplains

---

[49] Alvah Hovey, *A Memoir of the Life and Times of Isaac Backus* (Boston: Gould and Lincoln, 1858), p. 202.
[50] Cathcart, p. 66.

were among the most prominent and useful in the army."[51] He certainly held at least one chaplain in the highest possible regard—his personal chaplain, John Gano.

## The Forgotten Battle: The Baptists And The Battle Of King's Mountain

Colonel Patrick Ferguson, a British commander, arrived in North Carolina in early September 1780. He was on a quest to raise more troops for a Loyalist militia. He was expected to provide protection to Lord Cornwallis' flank, as Cornwallis was directing the main body of the army.

Hearing of the threat of an attack from local militia, Ferguson demanded the patriots to lay down their arms or face the consequences. In addition, he caught wind of forces over the Tennessee mountains that were poised to come in and attack him. These were none other than the Baptist Regulators who had been displaced by the wicked William Tryon after Alamance. He responded to them with a harsh warning, which in essence stated that if they attempted such an attack that he would march his men over the mountains and slaughter them. This warning would not dissuade the Baptists.

On October 7, 1780, a largely Baptist contingent, affectionately remembered as the "Overmountain

---
51 Ibid, p. 42

Men," defeated a British force at King's Mountain. These men came from Virginia, North Carolina, South Carolina, Georgia, and what would later become Tennessee. The latter group, a largely Baptist group of frontiersmen, walked almost non-stop for over eleven days to this battle. The importance of this victory at King's Mountain is recorded for us by Jeffrey J. Crow in his book *Chronicle of North Carolina during the American Revolution:*

> In response to the impudent threat, frontiersmen from Virginia, North Carolina, South Carolina, Georgia, and what later became Tennessee joined forces to attack the British army. Ferguson retreated to King's Mountain and camped atop its steep slopes, some one-and-one-half miles from the North Carolina border. In a brilliant four-pronged attack, the undisciplined and untrained militia captured the mountain while inflicting heavy losses on the enemy. Ferguson was killed. The victory was all the more remarkable because the military force had proceeded without the leadership or guidance of the state or of the Continental Line.[52]

Ferguson made some bad decisions, for sure. He made his truly fatal mistake when he arrived on top of the mountain and boasted, "I am the king of this

---

52 Crow, p. 43.

# LAID BY THE BAPTISTS

mountain and God Almighty Himself could not drive me from it."[53] Maybe never has one's words tasted so bitter, when one was forced to eat them! And to Ferguson, the author wishes to express a belated, and yet timely, "bon appetit!"

## After King's Mountain

Immediately after their duty was fulfilled at King's Mountain, the Overmountain Men would rush back across the mountains to defend their homes from the attacking Indians. The Revolutionary War would soon come to a close, but the valiant Baptists of Tennessee would continue defending their families and battling for the souls of men.

Tidence Lane, who was like a son to the famed Ole' Shubal Stearns, organized Tennessee's first Baptist church by 1779. Baptists would then tear across Tennessee like a holy wild fire for decades to come!

## A Military Miracle

The Battle of King's Mountain should be remembered as one of the most startling military happenings of all time! When in history has an army, that didn't exist, come together to fight an important battle to absolute victory, with such odds stacked

---

[53] John S. Pancake, *The Destructive War* (Tuscaloosa: University of Alabama Press, 1985), p. 118.

against them? This was a "David and Goliath" story to be sure! The Overmountain Men had inferior weapons, inferior training, inferior organization, and an inferior position on the field of battle. They had to fight uphill, after having walked many days with very little rest. The army then dispersed, never to assemble again in such an arrangement.

The only thing that could possibly trump these facts in history is the unfathomable truth that had this not happened, the entire Revolution may have been lost.

## The Battle Of King's Mountain, Extremely Significant

After having read many books about the Overmountain Men and the Battle at King's Mountain, having visited and conducted tours on these hallowed grounds on several occasions, and having lectured about this battle in countless churches and colleges, the author is of the bedrock conviction that the significance of this battle has been grossly under-emphasized by historians and hidden from God's people by Satan. This must be the case, for even if modern historians don't choose to render a proper assessment after analyzing the historical record one would still think that the words of a man such as Thomas Jefferson would shape the thought pattern of the historians. After all, he was alive and well during this period and had a brilliant mind in every possible sense.

## Thomas Jefferson Quote, Monumental

Thomas Jefferson wrote, "I remember well the deep and grateful impression made on the minds of every one by that memorable victory. It was the joyful annunciation of that turn of the tide of success which terminated the Revolutionary War, with the seal of our independence."[54]

## How Does One Process This Jeffersonian Quote?

Senator James T. Broyhill, in the foreword to Randell Jones' book *Before They Were Heroes at King's Mountain*, writes succinctly:

> "If there had been no victory at Kings Mountain, there would have been no battle at The Cowpens. And if there had been no victory at Cowpens, there would have been no battle at Guilford Courthouse. And if there had been no Battle of Guilford Courthouse, there would have been no Yorktown and no surrendering of the British troops under General Lord Cornwallis. The victory at Kings Mountain initiated a chain of events that ended with America's freedom.

---

54 Randell Jones, *Before They Were Heroes at King's Mountain* (Winston-Salem: Daniel Boone Footsteps, 2011), p. 17 of Foreword.

> This victory was secured by the brave backwoodsmen and Overmountain Patriots who enjoyed a reputation that had grown in notoriety, legend, and respect."[55]

## Did I Hear That Right?

Yes, dear reader, the Revolution was not only sparked by Baptists in North Carolina who were fighting a revolution long before Concord and Lexington, but the Revolution's tide was turned by a militia composed of frontiersmen. Among the ranks of those frontiersmen were hordes of Baptists that had been produced as a result of the Separate Baptist Revival.

This is not to say that all Overmountain Men were Baptists, for not all were believers of any rank. However, the record is clear that a large part of them were Baptists, and were indeed returning to fight another day after their defeat ten years previous at Alamance Creek.

---

[55] Ibid, p. 16

# Conclusion

## American Foundations Were Laid By *The Baptists*

To briefly summarize all that has been presented in this short treatise: if you could remove the spiritual, political, and Revolutionary contributions that the Baptists have made from the history of the colonies and America, this land may not even resemble the land so many of you have come to appreciate and love.

Next, to consider that the same great God, Jesus Christ, who used his Baptist people to accomplish all that is herein written and then sovereignly defended the United States through all of her wars and woes is supremely humbling. Indeed, America was no accident!

It is the prayer of the author that this great land will continue to honor the Baptist principles upon which she was founded. May Baptist churches be birthed and fill this land, and may the Baptist people be willing to defend this nation against grave threats to our liberty, whether those threats come from without or from within!

# Afterword

**Why Didn't I Know**

That's a good question. Surely every Baptist and every history student should at least know a good bit of this information. Some things are abundantly clear.

**The first-** is that the Devil hates the scriptural churches of Jesus Christ, and so he hides from the Baptists their testimony. He knows that when people get attached to their roots it can be a dangerous tool that is used against him. He doesn't want people to know God used the Baptists in the past, because he doesn't want the Baptists to believe they could be used today. He doesn't want Baptists to know that the principles of civil government and specifically the principles of American liberty were derived from the Baptists, introduced into the colonies by the Baptists, and defended by the Baptists, lest Baptists realize that it is vital for them as a people to defend these principles today.

Truly, when Baptists are given back their own history, they draw inspiration, zeal, and encouragement from it. They say things like, "Wow, God used Baptist people to shape this nation before, maybe if we obey and trust Him today, He will use us in a mighty way in our generation." The devil will fight to keep this from becoming the prevailing mindset. He is happy now with so many Baptists viewing themselves as powerless grasshoppers in a land of pagan giants.

**The second thing that is abundantly clear-** is that if God's people do not preserve and teach their own heritage to the next generation, no one will! This book grew out of a broken heart. The author for many years has traveled the country teaching and preaching the Gospel and Baptist heritage. There have been some others in recent years that have aided in this monumental task. The fact remains: Baptist young people are continuing to depart their churches and are going into the pagan, false Christian societies or are going nowhere at all. It is clear that people who think they are just another flavor of a Protestant church out of the many dozens of choices will very seldom turn out to be a dedicated, separated, holy servant of Christ. They are spiritually dying to get their own identity and heritage. But who will give it to them?

## Consider the Scripture

In Psalm 78 the Lord admonished Israel to make sure that their children would be passed on not just the Word of God but also the stories of the mighty acts of God in their history. Five generations are mentioned in this passage. God has done all the mighty things recorded in this book. Yes, He used His men, but to Him alone belongs the glory. If you have benefited from this book, pass it along to someone else, so they too can know the true history of America and the Baptist people.

Carefully consider the following passage of Scripture:

## Psalm 78:1-8

Give ear, O my people, to my law:
incline your ears to the words of my mouth.
I will open my mouth in a parable:
I will utter dark sayings of old:
Which we have heard and known,
and our fathers have told us.
We will not hide them from their children,
shewing to the generation to come
the praises of the Lord, and his strength,
and his wonderful works that he hath done.
For he established a testimony in Jacob,
and appointed a law in Israel,
which he commanded our fathers,
that they should make them known to their children:
That the generation to come might know them, even
the children which should be born;
who should arise and declare them to their children:
That they might set their hope in God,
and not forget the works of God,
but keep his commandments:
And might not be as their fathers,
a stubborn and rebellious generation; a generation
that set not their heart aright, and whose spirit was not
stedfast with God.

# Works Cited

Backus, Isaac, *History of New England*, Vol. 1, (Paris: The Baptist Standard Bearer, 1871, reprinted)

Benedict, David, *A General History of the Baptist Denomination in America*, (Boston: Manning and Loring, 1813)

Butterfield, Lyman H., *Elder John Leland, Jeffersonian Itinerant*, (Worcester: American Antiquarian Society, 1952)

Cathcart, William, *The Baptist Encyclopedia*, (Philadelphia: Louis H. Everts, 1883)

Cathcart, William, *The Baptists and the American Revolution*, (Lansing: Calvary Publishing, reprint, 1876)

Clarke, John, *Ill Newes from New England*, (London: Henry Hills, 1652)

Crow, Jeffrey J., *A Chronicle of North Carolina During the American Revolution 1768-1789*, (Raleigh: North Carolina Division of Archives and History, 1975)

Dalton, Robert, *Struggle for Liberty: The Baptists, The Bible and Church-State Conflict in Colonial America*, (Bloomington: Author House, 2004)

Dawson, Joseph Martin, *Baptists and the American Republic*, (New York: Arno Press, 1980)

Edwards, Morgan, "Materials North Carolina," unpublished manuscript.

Estep, William Roscoe, *Revolution Within the Revolution: The First Amendment in Historical Context, 1612-1789*, (Grand Rapids: Wm. B. Eerdmans Publishing Co., 1990)

Hendricks, Garland A., *Saints and Sinners*, (Thomasville: Charity and Children, 1964)

Hovey, Alvah, *A Memoir of the Life and Times of Isaac Backus*, (Boston: Gould and Lincoln, 1858)

Jones, Randell, *Before They Were Heroes at King's Mountain*, (Winston-Salem: Daniel Boone Footsteps, 2011)

King James Bible

Leland, in a letter from the undated *Madison Papers*, cited by Butterfield in ibid

Little, Lewis Peyton, *Imprisoned Preachers and Religious Liberty in Virginia*, (Lynchburg: J. P. Bell Co., 1938)

Lumpkin, William L., *Baptist Foundations in the South*, (Reprinted, Ashville: Revival Literature, 2006)

Nelson, Wilbur, *The Hero of Aquidneck: A Life of Dr. John Clarke*, (Grand Rapids: Fleming H. Revell, 1998)

*North Carolina Baptist Historical Papers, II* (April, 1898)

Pancake John S., *The Destructive War,* (Tuscaloosa: University of Alabama Press, 1985)

Paschal, George W., *History of North Carolina Baptists*, Vol. 1, (Raleigh: General Board of North Carolina Baptist State Convention, 1930)

Semple, Robert Baylor, *A History of the Rise and Progress of the Baptists in Virginia,* (Richmond: published by the author, printed by John O'Lynch, 1810)

Sprague, William Buell, *Annals of the American Pulpit: Baptists,* (New York: Robert Carter and Brothers, 1860)

Whitefield, George, *George Whitefield's Journals* (Guilford and London: Banner of Truth, Billing and Sons, Ltd., 1960)

Virginia Declaration of Rights (June 12, 1776), Article XVI

*Sandy Creek 1802 building*

*Site of Sandy Creek's first church service*

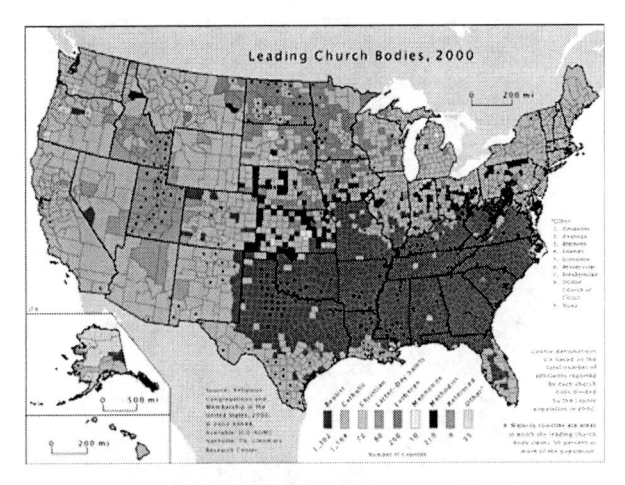

*Map depicting the saturation of the
South with conservative Baptists*

*Portsmouth Compact*

*John Clarke's Rhode Island Charter*

*Rhode Island Statehouse where the words from the charter are etched into the marble*

# LAID BY THE BAPTISTS 101

*Gravesite of Obadiah Holmes*

*Statue of Mary Dyer outside of the
Massachusetts statehouse in Boston*

*Words from Mary Dyer's monument*

*Sign at Alamance Battlefield*

# LAID BY THE BAPTISTS 103

*Monument at Alamance Battlefield*

*Hillsborough hanging site*

*Marker at Hillsborough hanging site*

*Marker 2 for Hillsborough hanging site*

# LAID BY THE BAPTISTS 105

*Sycamore Shoals Fort, mustering site
for the Overmountain Men*

*Baptist minister Matthew Talbot's cabin inside the
fort at Sycamore Shoals*

# American Foundations

**KING'S MOUNTAIN SOLDIERS**

Lane, Richard
Lane, Tidence
Lane, Aquilla
Lane, William
Lane, Jesse
Lane, Charles
Lane, James
Lane, John
Lane, Samuel
Landrum, James
Landrum, Thomas
Langston, John
Langston, Robert
Lankford, John
Lankford, Benjamin
Lannim, Joseph
Large, Joseph

*Tidence Lane's family members listed in Overmountain Men book as some of the many Baptist soldiers who fought in the Battle of King's Mountain*

*King's Mountain monument*

*Overmountain Men monument*

*Overmountain Men marker*

*Colonel Patrick Ferguson marker*

*View looking up towards the top of King's Mountain*

# LAID BY THE BAPTISTS

## Shoot Tree to Tree

*Ben Hollingsworth and myself took right up the side of the mountain, and fought our way from tree to tree, up to the summit. I recollect I stood behind one tree and fired until the bark was nearly all knocked off, and my eyes pretty well filled with it. One fellow shaved me pretty close, for his bullet took a piece out of my gun stock. Before I was aware of it, I found myself apparently between my own regiment and the enemy, as I judged by seeing the paper the Whigs wore in their hats and the pine twigs the Tories wore in theirs....*

Thomas Young, 16 years old, South Carolina patriot

*Plaque from the Overmountain Men museum conveying the spirit of the soldiers*

*Huge monument at King's Mountain battle site*